THIS BOOK IS NOT TO BE READ BY ANYONE YOUNGER THAN 8

THE SECRETS INSIDE THIS BOOK ARE ONLY FOR 8-YEAR-OLDS!

★ 8 ★

EVERYTHING YOU NEED TO KNOW WHEN YOU ARE

NEW YORK TIMES BESTSELLING AUTHOR

KiRSTeN MiLLeR

ILLUSTRATED BY ELLEN DUDA

AMULET BOOKS • NEW YORK

Cataloging-in-Publication Data has been applied for
and may be obtained from the Library of Congress.

ISBN 978-1-4197-4230-9

Text copyright © 2020 Kirsten Miller
Illustrations copyright © 2020 Ellen Duda
Book design by Ellen Duda

Printed and bound in China
10 9 8 7 6 5 4 3 2 1

Amulet Books are available at special discounts when purchased in quantity
for premiums and promotions as well as fundraising or educational use.
Special editions can also be created to specification. For details, contact
specialsales@abramsbooks.com or the address below.

ABRAMS The Art of Books
195 Broadway, New York, NY 10007
abramsbooks.com

FOR GEORGIA AND HER COUSINS ZOE, ROWAN, RILEY AND RHYS—
THE COOLEST, CRAZIEST, AND MOST DELIGHTFULLY
DISGUSTING KIDS I'VE EVER HAD THE PLEASURE TO KNOW

THIS IS A BOOK FOR
EVERYONE
TURNING
8

CONGRATULATIONS!!!

I hope you're excited, because this is going to be an **AWESOME** year. You've felt pretty grown-up for a while now, but 8 is when you start getting the respect you deserve! Little kids are going look up to you. Adults will begin treating you differently (finally!). You're going to discover lots of new things, pull lots of pranks—and probably get in some trouble. When you do, this book will be there for you. It's going to help you make sure 8 is the absolute best it can be—and get you ready for year number 9!

A FEW THiNGS EVERY 8-YEAR-OLD NEEDS

I've made a short list of things that might come in handy this year. You don't need to go out and buy anything. Borrow all the stuff you can. After all, you're only going to be 8 for one year. When you turn 9, put it all in a box and pass it down to the coolest 8-year-old you know.

A FEW STICK-ON MOUSTACHES
(they're not just for
upper lip hair anymore!)

A BOOK OF JOKES
(for sleepovers and
making new friends)

HAND SANITIZER
('cause life is gross)

A 800D HIDING SPOT
(for alone time)

A DISGUISE
(you never know when
you'll need one)

A TIE OR A SCARF
(for those times when
you need to impress adults)

A SQUIRT GUN
(for bathtub target practice)

A BAG OF GOOGLY EYES
(cause they're hilarious)

RUBBER CEMENT
(makes the best boogers)

A VERY REAL-LOOKING FAKE SPIDER
(for revenge)

A POPSICLE MOLD
(for making yourself
yummy treats)

A FAVORITE MONSTER
(for small talk with
other 8-year-olds)

HOW TO MAKE
BOOGERS
(WITHOUT USING YOUR NOSE)

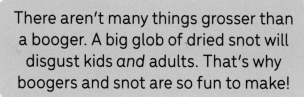

There aren't many things grosser than a booger. A big glob of dried snot will disgust kids *and* adults. That's why boogers and snot are so fun to make!

RUBBER CEMENT
AND GLUE BOOGERS

As soon as you discover rubber cement, art class will never be the same again! Spread some on a sheet of paper and let it dry. Then rub it with your finger. The rubber cement will ball up to create beautiful boogers!

Smaller boogers are more believable, but if you have the time (and enough rubber cement) feel free to make the biggest booger ever known! Regular glue can make boogers, too, but they won't be quite as brown and lovely.

GUM BOOGERS

Chewing gum doesn't make the best-looking boogers. But it *will* stick to almost anything, including walls, school desks, and the skin right below your nose.

Just use a magic marker or a teensy bit of food coloring to make your booger brown, green, or yellow (your choice!). Then stick it somewhere it will be spotted. (Keep it away from your hair and clothes!)

WiLL STICK ANYWHERE!!

SNOT YOU CAN EAT

There is one thing that's much, much grosser than boogers. That's snot you can eat. All you need to make it are 3 things: **WATER, GELATIN,** and **CORN SYRUP.**

Have an adult heat up half a cup of water.

Then stir in 3 tablespoons of gelatin and mix it well.

Use a drop of food coloring to make it nice and colorful.

Then slowly add in some corn syrup until your snot is as thick and disgusting as you want it to be!

NOW THAT YOU'RE 8, TRY EATING NEW THINGS

No, I'm not talking about boogers.
That's gross.

I'm going to tell you a secret. For most of my life, I refused to eat eggs. Everything about them grossed me out (especially where they come from). Then one day, not long ago, I finally gave in and decided to nibble a hard-boiled egg. And you know what? I *loved* it. Now I eat eggs whenever I can!

There are probably a few foods you couldn't stand when you were little. But that doesn't mean you won't like them now. People's taste buds change as we get older. (Mine did!) Why not give the foods you used to hate another try?

While you're at it, challenge yourself! Taste a few things you wouldn't usually eat. Some of the most amazing foods are the ones that seem the most revolting. Snails? *Awesome.* Octopus? *Divine.* Crickets? *Delightfully crunchy.* (Yes, I am totally serious.)

EATING NEW THINGS IS A GREAT WAY TO LOOK COOL

Let's imagine a special guest comes to your school to talk about foods from around the world. He brings a big plate of fried crickets for your class to try. Do you want to be the kind of kid who screams *EWWWW* and throws up? Or would you rather be the brave kid who picks one up and gives it a taste?

NEW FOODS MAKE EATING AN ADVENTURE

I once knew a kid who ate good old mac and cheese every day. That kid didn't know it, but she was bored out of her mind. Look, you're 8 years old. You're probably not ready to travel the world all by yourself. But whenever you bite into a new food, it's like setting off on an adventure. Your tongue will visit new places with every new dish that you try!

YOU NEVER KNOW WHAT YOU'RE GOING TO LIKE!

My favorite fruit, the rambutan, is covered in weird purple hair. It looks more like something you'd keep as a pet than something you'd want to put in your mouth. If I hadn't tried it, I would never have discovered how much I LOVE IT. So do your best to try new stuff—no matter how ugly it may be. Maybe you'll hate it. But maybe, just maybe, you'll discover your favorite food of all time!

RAMBUTAN

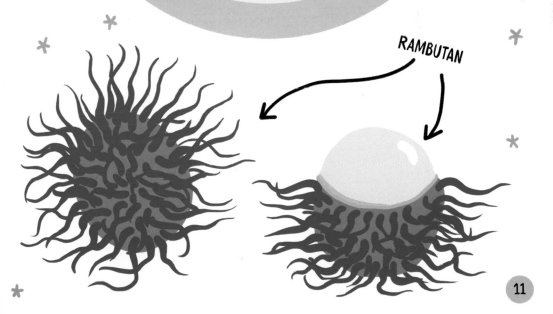

GET READY FOR SLEEPOVERS AND SLUMBER PARTIES

Maybe you are very sophisticated and you have already been invited to dozens of sleepovers and slumber parties. But for most of us, 8 is when the party starts. Go ahead and have a blast. You are going to remember these wild and crazy nights for the rest of your life.

Since you're just getting started, you're probably not sure what you'll need to bring—or what you'll do once you get there. Don't sweat it. I've got you covered!

WHAT YOU'LL NEED

Make sure you pack some comfortable pajamas, a toothbrush, and a change of clothes (you may be too tired to put them on in the morning, but it's good to have them just in case).

I RECOMMEND TAKING

A little treat for your friend's parents. Perhaps some flowers or cookies. It's not required, but it will make them like you. And you'd be surprised how much you can get away with after you've given someone a few tulips or a tasty cookie.

THINGS THAT WiLL MAKE IT A NiGHT TO REMEMBER

- Good jokes. If you can't remember any, find a beloved joke book and take it with you!

- Scary stories. Turn off the lights, grab a flashlight, and scare the pee out of each other.

- Fake mustaches. Always hilarious and surprisingly versatile! (See page 16.)

- The world's best pillow fort. (See page 18.)

- Sugar rushes. If your friend's parents are cool with it, make something suuuuuper sweet.

DARES AND PRANKS

These can be unbelievably fun. Just keep it safe, don't destroy your friend's house, and never be mean. Don't do anything to one of your friends that you wouldn't want done to you!

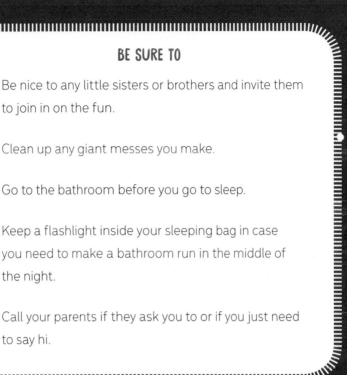

BE SURE TO

- Be nice to any little sisters or brothers and invite them to join in on the fun.

- Clean up any giant messes you make.

- Go to the bathroom before you go to sleep.

- Keep a flashlight inside your sleeping bag in case you need to make a bathroom run in the middle of the night.

- Call your parents if they ask you to or if you just need to say hi.

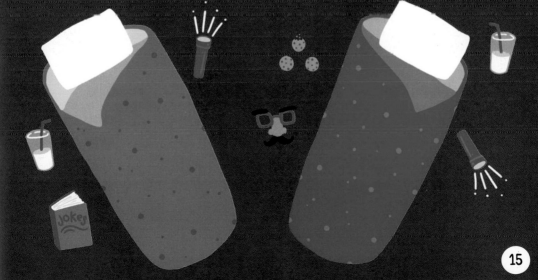

FOUR (MORE) REASONS

FAKE MUSTACHES

WILL ALWAYS BE AWESOME

So maybe you're one of those super cool kids who've been wearing fake mustaches since you were 5—and you're soooo over them.

Great! Then it's time to grab some scissors and get more creative! A couple of fake mustaches with sticky stuff on the back can supply you with at least 4 amazing new looks!

EAR HAIR

It may take people a while to realize you've sprouted ear hair, but I promise it will be worth the wait. They'll be horrified! Warning: DO NOT shove the hair into your ear hole. (Seriously!) Stick it right underneath, where you can reach it and everyone can see it.

NOSE HAIR

The only thing grosser than ear hair is nose hair! You don't need to shove it up your nose. (Again, shoving stuff in your ears or nose is a really bad idea. When I was your age, I had an orange seed stuck up my nose for days. It was NOT fun.) Just put a little patch of hair below each nostril. When you're done, add a fake booger or 2. Ah, perfection!

GIANT HAIRY MOLES

This is my favorite, and it's the easiest of all. Just cut a circle out of a fake mustache and put it wherever you want! A hairy mole right above the lip is a classic. But if you want to really shock people, stick one to your back when you go to the pool. (It will fall off in the water, but you'll get lots of laughs before you jump in.)

BUSHY EYEBROWS

Just cut your mustaches into the shape of eyebrows. Make them as thick or thin as you like!

HOW TO MAKE THE WORLD'S BEST FORT

At the age of 8, you should spend as much time as possible inside forts. They're warm, cozy, and perfect for sleepovers. But most importantly they're a great place to get away from parents and siblings!

A fort can turn even the most boring house into a magical world. With a little imagination, your fort can be:

A COZY IGLOO A FEW MILES AWAY FROM THE FROZEN NORTH POLE

A LOG CABIN IN THE MOUNTAINS THAT'S SURROUNDED BY BEARS

A SUBMARINE TRAVELING WITH A SCHOOL OF FISH ALONG THE OCEAN FLOOR

AN UNDERGROUND CAVE DECORATED BY TASTEFUL ELVES

A BURROW BUILT BY LARGE, CUDDLY BUNNIES

OR WHATEVER YOU WANT IT TO BE!

You can use almost anything to build your fort—chairs, beds and sofas all work. But if you want to make a fort that's nice and roomy and will last all day long, there's an easy way to do it . . .

USE A TABLE!

Dining room tables are perfect. Large desks can be great, too. Make sure the desk or table is against a wall. (So you'll have something to lean against!) Throw a few sheets over the top—and keep them in place with heavy books.

MAKE iT FEEL HOMEY

Cover the floor under the table with lots of pillows or couch cushions. (The more pillows, the better!) Add a few blankets, and you've got a cozy hideaway. If you want your fort to feel super magical, ask an adult if it's OK to hang up a string of Christmas or fairy lights inside.

THINGS YOU'LL WANT TO TAKE

Flashlights or glow sticks so you can see inside your awesome fort.

Cuddly pets like dogs and cats. Sorry, forts aren't for goldfish.

Friends—the more, the merrier!

Books and games to keep you entertained in your igloo/cabin/underground lair.

Snacks—bring enough so you won't have to leave your fort (unless you have to pee).

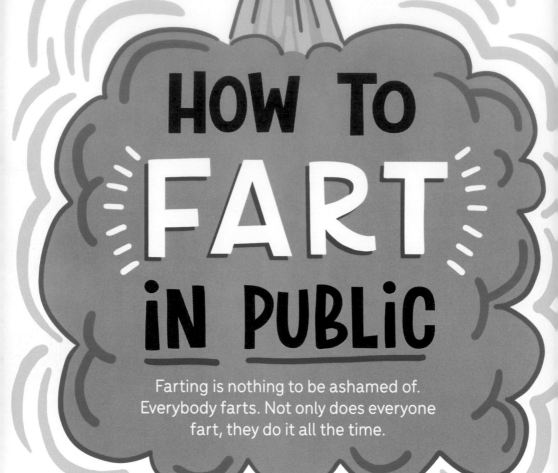

HOW TO FART IN PUBLIC

Farting is nothing to be ashamed of. Everybody farts. Not only does everyone fart, they do it all the time.

Most people fart somewhere between 10 and 20 times a day. Stop reading for a moment and look up from your book. Are there people around? If so, there's a pretty good chance that one of them is farting. You couldn't tell, right? That's because they were farting the right way.

IF YOU NEED TO FART...

It's hard to know if a fart is going to be super loud or smelly. The best thing to do is try to find a private place. When you're alone, you can fart any way you like. But sometimes you're stuck with a bunch of people nearby. So what do you do?

If you can, get up and walk around. This will spread the stink, and people won't be able to tell where it came from. If you're stuck in your seat, you're just going to have to do a little acting. Put on your best "innocent face" (see page 25). Then pray that your fart will be silent.

At some point in your life, probably at the very worst moment, you will let loose a loud, stinky fart in a room full of people. When that happens, there's only one thing you can do. Laugh your head off. Why not? After all, farts are hilarious, and as we all know, everyone farts.

THINGS THAT WILL MAKE YOU FART EVEN MORE

If you'd rather not fart in public, there are a couple of things you might want to avoid. You've probably heard that beans make you toot. That can be true, but beans are so good for you that they're worth a fart or 2. Instead, stay away from soda and chewing gum. They both make you swallow lots of air—which is often how farts get started!

HOW TO LOOK LIKE YOU DIDN'T DO IT

You just farted in public and everyone heard.
You can either have a good laugh . . .
or pretend it wasn't you.

Even if you don't go around farting in public, knowing
how to act innocent is a good skill to learn.

PUT ON YOUR INNOCENT FACE

Go look in the mirror. Have you done anything embarrassing or naughty in the last 5 minutes? No? Then this is how you look when you're totally innocent. Try to look exactly like this when you've farted.

DON'T PRETEND IT DIDN'T HAPPEN

Laugh along with everyone else—and then go right back to what you were doing before.

DON'T BLAME A FRIEND

That's just mean. But feel free to blame a dog or a baby if one is around. They fart all the time.

DON'T BE EMBARASSED

Even if everyone figures out it was you, who cares? Everyone farts—even cute little babies.

DON'T SAY, "WHO FARTED?"

The person who smells it first is usually the one who farted.

DON'T JUMP UP AND SHOUT, "IT WASN'T ME!"

Everyone will know that it was.

WHY CAN'T I CHEW WITH MY MOUTH OPEN?

Oh, but you can! When you're alone, you can chew with your mouth open all you want. Go ahead—knock yourself out! Let ketchup drip down your chin and little pieces of food fall out of your mouth.

But keep your mouth closed when you're around other people—including your friends and family. (Unless you're trying to gross out your brother or sister. It's totally acceptable to offer siblings a little "see food" when no one else is watching.)

Now that you're 8, there are a few things—like picking your nose or farting—that you should try to do in private. And chewing with your mouth open is at the top of the list. Why? Here are a few good reasons:

IT'S NASTY TO LOOK AT

I'm a big fan of gross stuff. (I just wrote a whole chapter on boogers!) But watching people chew with their mouths open makes me sick to my stomach. The last thing I want to see while eating a delicious fried chicken dinner is a big glob of meat, mashed potatoes, cole slaw, and spit inside someone else's mouth.

DON'T BELIEVE ME?

Then you need a demonstration. Ask a friend to chew with their mouth open in front of you. Make sure they've got a few different things mixed together in there. Now try to watch for 15 seconds. I bet you end up feeling a little bit sick!

PEOPLE WITH BAD MANNERS DON'T GET INVITED TO DINNER

You may now be eating dinner at your friends' homes more often. Chew with your mouth open and there's a chance you won't be invited back. So if you like eating with your friends' families, make sure your manners are good. Here are a few more helpful tips.

1. DON'T MAKE PEOPLE SICK TO THEIR STOMACHS.

2. DON'T COMPLAIN ABOUT THE FOOD.

3. DON'T MAKE BIG MESSES THE PARENTS HAVE TO CLEAN UP.

Follow these simple rules, and you'll be welcome wherever you go!

WHY iT'S NOT SMART

TO LIE

Everyone lies. It's true. I'm not going to lie to you! But that doesn't mean lying is ever the smart thing to do.

IF YOU LIE ALL THE TIME, PEOPLE WON'T TRUST YOU

Have you read the story "The Boy Who Cried Wolf"? If not, go read it right now! It's the tale of a boy who lied so much that no one believed him when he finally told the truth. And then he got eaten by a wolf.

"The Boy Who Cried Wolf" was written hundreds of years ago, and kids are STILL reading it! Why? Because it teaches an important lesson: If you lie all the time, you might have a hard time making people believe you when you really need them to. (Don't worry—wolves probably won't eat you.)

IT'S A LOT EASIER TO TELL THE TRUTH

When you tell a lie, you have to keep telling it. Let's say you tell some kids that your dad is Superman. You have to remember who you told and what EXACTLY you said—unless you want to be caught. It would be sooo much easier just to tell the truth so you don't have to keep making stuff up!

YOU CAN FIND A WAY TO TELL THE TRUTH WITHOUT HURTING FEELINGS

Sometimes people lie to avoid hurting other people's feelings. These aren't the worst kind of lies, of course. But if you're smart, you can find a way to be nice AND tell the truth! For example, if someone gives you a present you don't really like, you don't have to lie about how much you love it. Just say, "Thank you! It's so nice of you to get me a present." WHICH IS TOTALLY TRUE!

HOW TO MAKE CRAZY GOOD POPSICLES

So what if you're not anywhere near the stove? "The rules" shouldn't hold you back from making yourself delicious treats!

The first thing you're going to need is a popsicle mold. You should be able to get one at any discount store. I've seen them for as little as a dollar. So it may be something you can buy for yourself! The next thing you need is some creativity. Almost anything you like to drink (and a few things you like to eat) can be turned into amazing popsicles. Come up with a great recipe, and you may be able to sell your creations on the next hot day!

CHOCOLATE MILK, YOGURT, OR PUDDING

Want popsicles that taste like ice cream? Try filling your molds with any of these ingredients! At my house, yogurt is our #1 favorite. We pour vanilla yogurt into our molds and throw in a few blueberries and raspberries for gorgeous red, white, and blue popsicles.

LEMONADE OR JUICE

These are classic popsicle ingredients. Any kind of juice is going to make a great popsicle, but why not jazz it up a bit? Throw some berries or sliced kiwis in the mold before you pour in the juice! Your popsicles will be tasty AND beautiful.

BANANAS

No popsicle mold yet? Do you have any bananas? Fantastic! Take off the banana peels, shove a popsicle stick in one end, and roll the bananas in yogurt or chocolate syrup. Add a few nuts or sprinkles if you like. Then put your banana in the freezer (on a plate, of course). Leave it there for an hour. Then eat!

FRESH FRUIT OR SMOOTHIES

Popsicles made out of fresh fruit or smoothies are delicious, and your parents may let you eat as many as you like. Some kinds of fruit, like cantaloupe and watermelon (super yummy) can be mushed up with a fork and shoved into a popsicle mold. If you're in the mood for smoothie popsicles, ask your mom or dad for help mixing a bunch of different fruits in a blender.

33

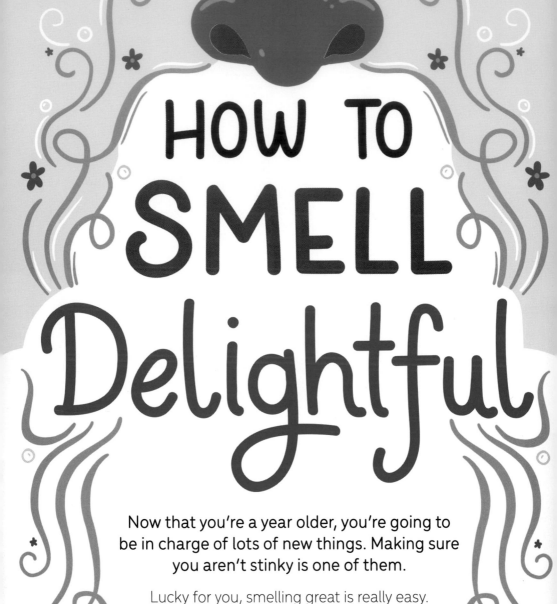

HOW TO
SMELL
Delightful

Now that you're a year older, you're going to be in charge of lots of new things. Making sure you aren't stinky is one of them.

Lucky for you, smelling great is really easy. You don't even need to buy anything!

HOP IN THE SHOWER
AND CLEAN YOUR BOOTY

Yeah, that's right. I said shower, not bath. Baths are great, of course. (There's a whole chapter in this book about them!) But you won't always have time for a nice, long soak. So jump in the shower and soap yourself up. Make sure you reach all those nooks and crannies (like your butt, ears, and toes). Wash your hair, too, if it needs it! 5 minutes is all it takes, and unless you end up wrestling a skunk, you should smell great for the rest of the day.

BRUSH YOUR TEETH

This is pretty important for lots of reasons (green teeth are gross, and cavities hurt), but it's also the best way to keep your breath from smelling like dog food.

DON'T BOTHER WITH PERFUMES OR COLOGNES

Clean 8-year-olds smell great without perfume. But if it's a special occasion and you want to smell extra great, look for some vanilla extract in your kitchen cupboard. (It usually comes in a little brown bottle.) Put a teensy bit on a finger and dab it behind your ears. It smells good on everyone—boys or girls.

WEAR CLEAN CLOTHES

If your jeans don't look or smell dirty, you can probably get away with wearing them a couple of times. But socks and underwear need to be changed EVERY day.

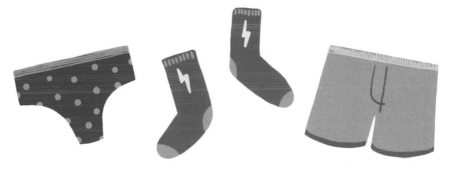

SPRINKLE A LITTLE POWDER IN YOUR SNEAKERS

Do people gag when you take off your shoes? Don't worry, smelly feet are very common and perfectly normal. There's also an easy way to keep them smelling fresh (or at least not totally disgusting). Just put a little bit of baby powder inside and shake it around.

HOW TO TAKE THE

Baths aren't just for soaping up your booty. A good bath is the perfect way to end a long, hard day. (It's also one of the easiest ways to keep smelling awesome.)

THE RIGHT MUSIC

What kind of bath would you like to take? The right music can make your bath relaxing, fun—even a little bit scary, if you're into that sort of thing. (I recommend some nice Hawaiian luau tunes.) Just make sure the phone or music player is placed somewhere secure away from the bath, so it can't fall into the water!

SWIM GOGGLES

Put on a pair of swim goggles and suddenly you're not soaking, you're swimming. Got any little plastic figurines? Fantastic! Throw them in the bottom and pretend you're a shark hunting for someone to eat.

SQUIRT GUNS

The bathtub is one of the very best places to improve your squirt-gun skills. Close the curtain (that part's important), set up a few targets along the edge of the tub, and see how many you can hit. No squirt gun? No worries! A regular old straw can be just as fun.

BEST BATH EVER

For the world's greatest bath, all you've gotta do is turn on the faucet, plug up the drain, and grab a few essential things . . .

A POPSICLE

A good bath is nice and warm. What better way to enjoy it than with a cold, refreshing popsicle? (See page 33.) You can't make a mess in the bathtub, and there's no one there to complain about your manners, so go ahead and slurp and spill all you like.

BUBBLES

I think we can all agree that bubbles make everything better. If you don't have any bubble bath handy, why not make your own? Just mix together a palm-sized dollop of body wash, an egg white, and a tablespoon of honey. (You might need some help with that egg.) Then pour it into the tub and get ready for bubbles!

PLASTIC POOP

If you can get your hands on some plastic poop, you can pull one of the most hilarious pranks of all time. Just leave it floating in the bathtub when you get out. The next person in the bathroom will be in for a big surprise!

SO WHAT'S THE BIG DEAL ABOUT PRIVATES?

Privates *aren't* a big deal. Everyone has them.
There's nothing gross or weird about them at all.
But there is a good reason they're called privates.
When you're a kid, they're not for sharing.

YOUR PRIVATES BELONG TO YOU

Your privates, like the rest of your body, belong to you and you only! You're the one in charge. Unless you're sick and a doctor needs to take a look, you should be the only person who gets to touch them.

IT'S YOUR JOB TO TAKE CARE OF THEM

If something down there itches, hurts, or feels a bit weird, be sure to tell a parent! Your privates are just like the rest of your body—sometimes they need medicine. It's no big deal to let a doctor take a look. That's their job! *Your* job is to make sure your body gets help when it needs it!

IT'S NOT A GOOD IDEA TO SHOW THEM OFF

Don't worry about hopping into the bath. Run around your room naked all you want. But you shouldn't share your privates with your friends or show them off. And never, ever take any pictures.

NO ONE ELSE SHOULD EVER TOUCH THEM

Unless you're sick or in a doctor's office, no one should touch your privates. If someone does, you should tell the adult you trust most right away. Don't be shy! This is very important, and you will NOT get in trouble for telling.

WHAT SHOULD YOU SAY WHEN SOMEONE ASKS YOU
WHAT YOU WANT TO BE WHEN YOU GROW UP?

It's a totally ridiculous question, isn't it?
When my sister was 8, she wanted to be a bear.
At your age, you shouldn't be expected to know
what you want to be! (If you do, that's awesome.
Best of luck to you, kid .)

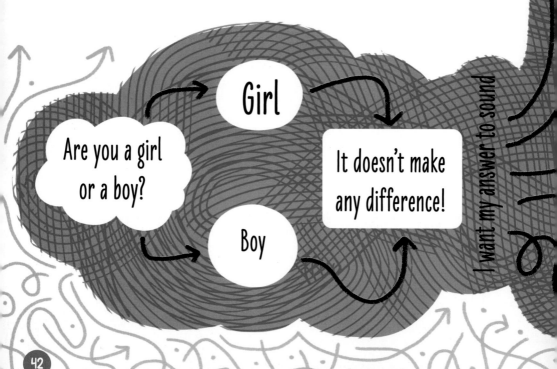

Are you a girl
or a boy?

Girl

Boy

It doesn't make
any difference!

I want my answer to sound

DO YOU REALLY HAVE TO GO TO BED AT THE SAME TIME EVERY NIGHT?

You're not sleepy and you have so many things you'd rather do! But your parents make you stick to the same boring bedtime. You're 8 now! Why can't you go to sleep when you want??

You've probably heard that not getting enough sleep is bad for you. And I'm sure you've stayed up past your bedtime once or twice and felt totally fine. But you didn't feel *great*, did you? See, that's the thing about sleep. Getting the right amount can make you feel absolutely *awesome*.

GET ENOUGH SLEEP AND YOU'LL BE SMARTER

No kidding! Sleep helps your brain develop and grow. Most 8-year-olds need between 10 and 11 hours of sleep every night. If you get that many hours, the next morning, your brain is going to be at its best. You'll be able to think better, remember more, and come up with funnier jokes.

YOUR BODY WILL FEEL STRONGER, FASTER, AND MORE POWERFUL

Not only is sleep amazing for your brain, it's great for the rest of you, too! In fact, you know who else tries to get more than 10 hours of sleep every night? Professional athletes, that's who! In fact, some of the most famous athletes in the world sleep more than 12 hours a night!

IT MAY KEEP YOU AWAY FROM DOCTORS

I can't make any promises. You're still going to need a shot or 2. But a good night's sleep can help protect you from illnesses like the cold. And that will help keep you out of the doctor's office!

YOUR PARENTS WILL BE MORE FUN

Parents need kid-free time. Sorry, but it's true! Don't take it personally. Someday you'll need adult time, too. If you give your parents a couple of hours to rest and relax, there's a good chance they won't be cranky in the morning—and they'll have more energy to have fun with you!

HOW TO CONVINCE ADULTS THAT YOU'RE SUPER MATURE

You're going to be a grown-up for most of your life. For now, just enjoy being 8. Make lots of poop jokes and play in the mud! But whenever you get tired of being treated like a kid, here are a few easy things you can do to seem more grown up.

START CONVERSATIONS

The easiest way to prove you're mature is by talking to adults. Unfortunately, most grownups ask kids the same boring questions over and over and over again. How's school? What's your favorite subject? Blah, blah, blah. So why not *start* some conversations instead? Ask adults if they'd like to visit Mars. Or what they think of mummies. Conversations are easy when you're talking about things that interest you!

LEARN A FEW INTERESTING FACTS

What *are* the things you find interesting? Maybe you love dogs. (Did you know their sense of smell is 100,000 times better than ours?) Giant squid are awesome, too. (Did you know their eyeballs are as big as Frisbees?) Memorize a few amazing facts about your favorite subject and share them during your conversations!

BEHAVE IN RESTAURANTS

It's pretty easy. Speak in a normal voice. Put your napkin in your lap. Don't make loud slurping noises or eat spaghetti with your fingers. Always be polite to the people serving your food. And for heaven's sake, chew with your mouth closed!

TAKE CARE OF YOUR PETS

This is one of the best ways to show how responsible you are. Make it your job to give your pets water and food. Take them for walks. And if you REALLY want to look mature, volunteer to deal with the poop!

BE SUPER NICE TO LITTLE KIDS

Want to look grown-up? Play with babies and younger kids. You'll seem so much older and more sophisticated than they do, and their parents will be grateful for the help. Plus it's good practice for babysitting, which can be a great job when you're a little bit older!

HELP OUT AROUND THE HOUSE

See if your dad needs help with the dishes. Take out the garbage without being asked. Give your mom a hand with the vacuuming. Who knows? If you're super lucky, maybe you can even earn some money if you go beyond the basics. And there's nothing more grown-up than having your own cash!

WEAR A TIE OR A SCARF

Seriously. I don't know why, but a scarf or a tie makes kids seem much more mature. Add a pair of eyeglasses and you might be mistaken for a short adult. Don't believe me? Just try it out!

HOW TO PACK YOUR OWN YUM BOX

Want to prove how grown up you are?
Pack your own lunch some day this week.
Put the right stuff in your yum box, and
you'll blow your parents' minds!

First you need a box or a bag. Then find a few little containers for the food. (Try to find ones that can be reused again!) Now you have to decide how to fill them. I know it's tempting to pack a bunch of chips and a cupcake. But a bag full of junk food will make you look like a little kid—and it could also make you barf during recess.

No, you need to pack food that's tasty and good for you. This is not hard to do! When you're 9, we'll talk about sandwiches (the perfect food). But for now, let's stick with what's already in your fridge. See if you can find each of the following:

SOMETHING VEGGIE

Adults love to put carrots in kids' lunchboxes. If you like carrots, that's great. But since you're packing this yum box, YOU GET TO CHOOSE! What's your favorite vegetable? Pickles, peas, broccoli, jicama? Toss some inside!

SOMETHING FRUITY

Same thing goes for fruit. You don't need to pack an apple or a banana. YOU GET TO CHOOSE! Pack whatever you like! (No, fruit-flavored candy does NOT count!)

SOMETHING WITH PROTEIN

Protein helps build muscles. It can be found in meat, eggs, yogurt, cheese, and beans. Which of those things do you like best? Go ahead and pack it!

SOMETHING GRAINY

Grains are things like wheat and rice. The ones that are brown instead of white are usually the best for you. You know what would go great with that cheese you just packed? Some crackers! Or how about some rice with those beans? Or you could go with my personal favorite—pretzels.

HOW TO HAVE TONS ~~~ OF ~~~ ENERGY

One of the great things about being 8 is having lots of energy. But there are still going to be times when you want just a little bit more.

There could be a game you want to win or a big performance you'd like to ace. You're going to need all the energy you can get! So what should you do?

GO OUTSIDE

You need sunlight! It helps your body make important vitamins—and it tells your brain that it's supposed to be awake. If you spend all day staring at screens, your body may have a hard time knowing when it's time to wake up or go to sleep.

TRY NOT TO HAVE A LOT OF SUGAR

You know how some kids go nuts when they eat sugar? (Maybe you're one of them!) That happens because the sugar in candy, sodas, and desserts gives them a rush of energy. But the rush ends pretty quickly, and when it does, they have less energy than ever.

GET A GOOD NIGHT'S SLEEP

If you want lots of energy, get lots of sleep! (See page 45 to learn more.)

EAT A BANANA INSTEAD

Bananas are delicious, and they're filled with vitamins and nutrients that will give you an energy boost that will last much longer.

DRINK PLENTY OF WATER

You should be drinking at least 5 glasses of water a day (and more when you're playing). If you don't get enough water, your whole body won't work as well as it should.

EXERCISE

Exercise keeps your body strong and working well—which will give you energy and makes you feel great!

HOW TO GET GERMS BEFORE THEY GET YOU

I'm sure you know about the teensy, tiny creatures known as "germs." You've probably heard that they're practically invisible, they're everywhere, and they're out to make you sick. I'm sorry to tell you that's all totally true.

But don't run away screaming just yet! Because these terrible little creatures are usually very easy to defeat—and the weapons you'll need can be found in most homes and schools.

SOAP AND WARM WATER

These 2 simple things are the perfect germ-killing combo. But they have to go together! Washing your hands with plain old water isn't going to do you much good. And washing your hands with just soap is sticky and gross.

TISSUES

Tissues don't really kill germs. They just trap them and keep the nasty little creatures from spreading. Use them when you have to sneeze—and throw them out right away.

HAND SANITIZER

I'm not a big fan of hand sanitizer. It kills bad germs, but it also gets rid of good germs, too. (Yes, there are good germs, and you want to keep them!) It's much better to wash your hands, but if you can't get to a restroom, a bit of hand sanitizer will do in a pinch.

FRUITS AND VEGETABLES

No, this isn't a trick to make you eat better! You know how your parents are always telling you that fruits and vegetables are "healthy?" Well they're right! Fruits and vegetables do lots of good things for your body, including protecting you from germs that manage to sneak up your nose (or down your throat)!

ALWAYS WASH YOUR HANDS AFTER TOUCHING...

POOP AND SNOT
(DUH)

TOILETS
(ESPECIALLY PUBLIC TOILETS)

THE INSIDE OF
YOUR NOSE

HAND RAILS OR
ELEVATOR BUTTONS

DEAD ANIMALS
(EVEN IF YOU'RE GOING TO EAT
THEM AFTER THEY'VE BEEN COOKED)

DIAPERS
(FOR THOSE OF YOU WITH BABY
BROTHERS OR SISTERS)

SUBWAY POLES

GARBAGE CANS

YOUR BUTT

YOUR SHOES

SNAKES
(EVEN PET SNAKES CAN
CARRY BAD GERMS)

MONEY
(BELIEVE IT OR NOT, MONEY MAY
BE THE GROSSEST THING OF ALL)

YOUR PRIVATES

LIVE ANIMALS
(INCLUDING CUTE LITTLE GERBILS)

HOW TO PICK YOUR FAVORITE MONSTER

By the age of 8, you should definitely know who your favorite monster is! In case you don't, this handy chart can help you figure it out. If you want a monster who's a little less famous (but just as awesome), check out the next chapter!

I LIKE MY MONSTERS . . .

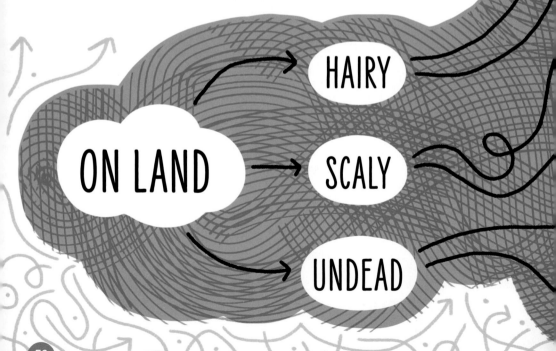

ON LAND → HAIRY

ON LAND → SCALY

ON LAND → UNDEAD

BAD SMELL
- Grunts a lot → BIGFOOT
- Speaks human
  - Might be someone you know → WEREWOLF
  - Not too bright → OGRE

HORRIBLE SMELL
- Lives in a cave → ABOMINABLE SNOWMAN
- Lives in a swamp → SKUNK APE

FIRE BREATHING
- Wings → DRAGON
- Amphibian → GODZILLA

BAD BREATH
- Cool hair → MEDUSA
- Goat sucking → CHUPACABRA

KINDA CUTE → VAMPIRE

TOTALLY ROTTEN → ZOMBIE

IN WATER

MIGHT EAT YOU

- Catchy nickname → **LOCH NESS MONSTER**
- Not as nice as they look → **MERPEOPLE**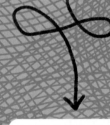

WILL DEFINITELY EAT YOU

- Enormous teeth → **JAWS**
- Tentacles
  - REAL! → **GIANT SQUID**
  - WHO KNOWS! → **KRAKEN**

A FEW (MAYBE) REAL MONSTERS YOU SHOULD GET TO KNOW

There are no monsters in your closet of under the bed, of course. (They're too big to fit!) But some people believe there are monsters living deep in the woods or at the bottom of lakes. (FYI: None of these people are scientists.)

Am I one of the people who believe in monsters? You bet! I've never seen one. There's no proof that they exist at all. But it sure does make the world more interesting to think that strange and mysterious creatures might be out there!

GIANT BLACK CATS

In the United Kingdom, people claim to have spotted enormous black cats the size of panthers wandering through their farms and backyards. The most famous one was called the Beast of Exmoor. What's so weird about a giant black cat? If you looked out your window right now and saw one, you'd know!

SKUNK APE

The Skunk Ape is a creature that may live in swamps right here in the United States. It's been spotted most often in Florida. It's smaller than Bigfoot and much less famous. Most people smell it before they see it—which is how it got its name. Fun fact: Its favorite food is lima beans.

YOWIE

There are lots of Bigfoot-like creatures all over the world. In the Australian Outback, they have the Yowie. It's a tall, hairy creature with giant feet. Like Bigfoot, the Skunk Ape, and other similar "monsters," Yowies do their best to avoid human beings, which probably means they're highly intelligent.

CHAMP

You've likely heard of the Loch Ness Monster in Scotland. (If you haven't, run to the library and check out a book on it right now!) But you may not know that the United States has giant lake monsters, too! The most famous lives in Lake Champlain, and it goes by the name of Champ. Some people who've seen it say it looks like an extinct dinosaur called a plesiosaur!

WHAT KIND OF CREATURES HAVE BEEN SNEAKING AROUND MY HOUSE?

It doesn't matter if you live in the middle of the woods or the middle of a big city (like I do). There's a very good chance that there are animals sneaking around your house late at night.

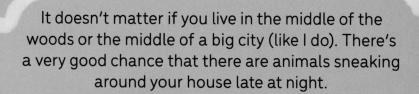

If you spot little footprints (or even gigantic ones), see if you can match them to one of the pictures below. So far, I've found cat, dog, opossum, and raccoon tracks outside my house. If my dreams come true, someday I'll find Bigfoot's, too!

CAT

DOG

COYOTE

RACCOON

SQUIRREL

WILD PIG

RABBIT

OPOSSUM

BIGFOOT

CHUPACABRA

MOUNTAIN LION

HOW TO HANDLE CUTE
(OR WONDERFULLY ICKY)
LITTLE CREATURES

I'm talking about toads, frogs, lizards, fireflies, beetles, turtles, tarantulas, pixies, crawdads, caterpillars, and all the other little things you may find in your yard.

1. GET TO KNOW THEM BEFORE YOU CATCH THEM

When I was 8, I wanted to catch every toad, lizard, and craw-dad I saw. I chased fireflies, hunted lizards, and collected frog's eggs. Later, I found out that it's not always a good idea to catch little animals—no matter how cute and harmless they may seem. Some (like fireflies) won't live long if you catch them. Others (like toads) may not be safe to touch. The best thing to do is to take out a book from the library to find out which little creatures are OK to catch!

2. HANDLE LITTLE THINGS WITH CARE

The last thing you want to do is hurt something so small. So you're going to need to be SUPER careful. Imagine if a giant decided to play with you. It would have to be really gentle—or else you'd get squished. And that would be really gross.

3. LET THEM GO

I'll bet you'd love a new pet. Maybe you want something cute and lovable. Or maybe (like me) you'd prefer a pet that will terrify your friends and family. But most animals you find outside will not be happy (or healthy) *inside*. Think about it—how would you feel if someone stuck you in a jar? Do these creatures a favor and let them go home!

4. WASH YOUR HANDS!

I know I probably sound like your mom. But your mom is right! Little creatures can be covered in germs that you definitely don't want to get in your mouth. So wash your hands as soon as you can get to a sink after handling small creatures!

LiTTLE THiNGS THAT COULD HURT YOU

FUZZY CATERPiLLARS

Most caterpillars are safe, but there are a few you definitely don't want to touch! It's a good idea to read a book about caterpillars before you even think about picking one up. One thing you'll find out fast—you never, ever want to touch caterpillars that look fuzzy or hairy. Those hairs can give you a nasty sting!

WHEEL BUGS

Nothing is more fun than catching bugs and having a good look at them under a magnifying glass. But there are a few you don't want to touch! Wheel bugs are just the kind of weird bugs I might have picked up when I was 8. Good thing I never saw one—the bite of a wheel bug can be worse than a bee sting!

TOADS

Yes, I know. This is very disappointing news. Toads are awesome, but they are also poisonous. Those warts on their skin? They aren't contagious. (You won't catch a case of warts from a toad!) But they do have poison inside of them that can be bad for your skin.

SCORPiONS, CENTiPEDES, SNAKES, AND SPIDERS

I probably don't need to warn you about these creatures. They look scary enough to frighten most of us away! But even if you're not scared at all, don't mess with them. Instead, find an adult and let them take a look. It may be something you don't want anywhere near your house!

LITTLE THINGS YOU COULD HURT WITHOUT KNOWING IT

FROGS, SALAMANDERS, AND NEWTS

Even when you think your hands are clean, they may have stuff on them (like sunscreen) that can hurt little wild creatures with soft, moist skin. Some frogs can be pets, but it's best not to touch the ones you find in your yard.

THINGS IT'S OK TO TOUCH IF YOU'RE CAREFUL

GECKOS

These super cute little lizards are safe to touch. Just be very gentle! BTW, there are only two venomous lizards in the Americas—the Gila monster and the Mexican beaded lizard. Wild iguanas can bite and shouldn't be messed with. But other lizards aren't going to hurt you!

CRAWDADS

Otherwise known as crawfish, these little lobster lookalikes can be found hiding under creek rocks. It's OK to catch them. It's even OK to eat them! But they probably taste terrible raw.

ALMOST ALL BEETLES

In North America, blister beetles, stag beetles, and longhorned beetles can bite. (Though none are very dangerous.) Find pictures of these beetles so you can recognize and stay away from them. Other beetles are OK to touch!

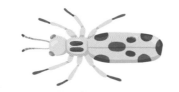

HOW TO WiN HALLOWEEN

Are you a little weird?
(Deep inside, we all are.)
Then Halloween is your time to shine!

You'll need an amazing costume to "win" Halloween. But I promise—all the hard work will be worth it. There aren't any prizes (unless you enter a contest), but your pride will last the entire year! Here's what you've got to do:

START PLANNiNG IN SEPTEMBER

If you want to win, you've got to take Halloween seriously! As soon as the weather starts getting cooler, you better get moving!

COME UP WiTH A NEW iDEA

You need a costume that no one on earth (or at least no one on your street) has ever thought of before!

DON'T SPEND A LOT OF MONEY

If you spend a million dollars on a costume, it's gonna look pretty awesome. But the *less* money you spend, the more impressed everyone will be. You win Halloween by having big brains—not big bucks.

YOU HAVE TO MAKE IT YOURSELF

Store-bought costumes are fine. But you won't win Halloween wearing one. Why? 'Cause half the kids in your neighborhood will be wearing the same thing. Don't worry—you won't need to learn how to sew or weld to make your own costume. Most of the time you can come up with something awesome using things you already own! (And probably a lot of glue.) Oh, and getting help from your family is totally fine!

BE SCARY

For goodness sake, this is the WHOLE POINT of Halloween. So if you're a fairy, be an evil fairy. If you're a lumberjack, be an evil lumberjack. Even unicorn costumes look a million times better with a plastic axe and some tastefully applied fake blood.

FUNNY *AND* SCARY
IS ALWAYS A WiNNER

If your costume can make people scream AND crack up, you will win the prize every time.

DON'T HAVE TIME THIS YEAR?

Maybe this year you were too busy making all those awesome popsicles to get started on your costume. You're going to have to get a costume from the store. If so, may I make a suggestion? Get 5 of your friends to buy THE SAME costume and go trick or treating together. There's nothing as scary (or funny) as 6 Spider-men or 6 identical princesses showing up at your door.

DON'T GET RID OF THAT
HALLOWEEN COSTUME!

Halloween night was a blast. You terrified your town, demanded treats from your neighbors, and passed out with chocolate smeared all over your face.

On November 1, you wake up to see your beloved costume in a pile on the floor. You worked your butt off making it and last night it brought you such pride! Now you're not sure what to do with it. I mean, it's not like your parents will let you wear it to school! (Parents can be so boring!)

IF IT'S SCARY, SAVE IT

A costume that's scary on Halloween is going to be EVEN SCARIER the other 364 days of the year. Why? Because if it's not Halloween, no one is expecting to see a kid in a costume! It will be absolutely perfect for pranks. All you'll have to do to freak people out is put it on and hang out in your front yard.

CRAFT A DISGUISE

Are there parts of your costume that can be recycled? Makeup, wigs, hats, and fake scars can all come in handy when you need a disguise. (And who doesn't need a disguise from time to time?)

PASS IT DOWN

If your costume was that awesome, spread the terror! Let another kid enjoy it next year! Donate it to a thrift store or give it to someone younger.

HOW TO MAKE
APRIL 1
THE SECOND-BEST
DAY OF THE YEAR

Halloween is the very best day of the year, of course! But April Fools' Day is another chance to show how funny, cool, and creative you can be!

April Fools' Day is a celebration that's at least 500 years old. It's the one day a year when everyone's allowed to pull pranks, make jokes, and fool everyone they know.

THERE ARE ONLY 3 RULES
1. BE CREATIVE
2. DON'T BE MEAN
3. DON'T DO ANYTHING DANGEROUS

WANT SOME SUGGESTIONS?

- Use a bar of white or clear soap to write a creepy message on the bathroom mirror. It will be invisible—until someone takes a shower. The steam will reveal the message when the person least expects it!

- Unscrew your friend's water bottle and cover the top with clear plastic.

- Put plastic bugs inside everyone's lunchboxes.

- Shove tissue paper into the tips of your siblings' shoes. (They'll think their feet grew overnight!)

- On little strips of paper, write "I SEE YOU" in creepy letters and hide the notes all over the house.

- Take the jacket off the book your mom is reading and put it on the weirdest book you can find.

- Add a little yogurt to your milk. It will look lumpy, as if it's gone bad. Show your parents. Then tell them you like it that way!

A FEW PERFECT PRANKS TO PLAY ON YOUR PARENTS

These easy pranks are perfect for moms and dads.
But if your parents are too wonderful to prank, don't
worry. These tricks work on other people, too!

PRO TIP:
NO MATTER HOW FUNNY THE PRANK IS, DON'T
PULL IT ON SOMEONE WHO'S IN A BAD MOOD!

GIVE YOUR FAMILY PICTURES A MAKEOVER

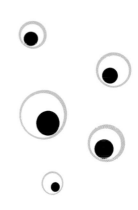

Get your hands on some googly eyes. Then wake up super early one morning—before anyone else is out of bed. Go around your house and find your framed family photos. Stick the googly eyes to the glass (never stick them to paper or you could rip the photos).

MMM, MMM MAYONNAISE

Get some Oreo cookies and scrape off all the cream. Then replace it with mayonnaise and offer your mom or dad a special treat! And that's not the only prank you can pull with mayonnaise! Put it on top of a cupcake, add some sprinkles, and pretend it's frosting

TOILET SPIDER

Take a black pen and head to the bathroom. Unroll the toilet paper a bit—but be careful not to rip it! Draw a black spider on the paper, and then roll it back up so the spider is hidden. The next time someone pulls off some paper, they'll see a giant black spider sitting on the roll!

WHAT TO DO IF YOU REALLY, REALLY, REALLY NEED SOME ATTENTION

You're 8, so you probably love attention. Some kids want more from their parents. Others want attention from their classmates. And a few want the whole wide world watching them.

But there are 2 different kinds of attention. There's good attention (which can come with applause and ice cream) and bad attention (which can lead straight to the principal's office). See, sometimes we want attention so badly that we do things that get us into trouble—or annoy the heck out of the people we want to impress. But it doesn't have to be that way! Here are a few tricks that will help you get the GOOD attention you deserve!

BE HELPFUL

A good way to get attention from someone is to offer to help them out! Ask your dad if you can help him make dinner. Ask your mom if you can help her feed her pet alligators. (Lucky you.) This works for friends, too! If one of your friends wants to be a ninja, offer to help her train! If another friend is in trouble for not cleaning his room, lend him a hand!

BE INTERESTING

If that sounds hard, it isn't. All you really have to do is talk! Find out what you share in common with the person whose attention you want. Maybe you both love unicorns. Maybe you both hate unicorns more than anything else. Once you know what you share in common, TALK ABOUT IT! (Just make sure you let the other person do at least half of the talking.)

BE FUNNY

Being funny is one of the best ways to get attention. If you can make people laugh, they'll love spending time with you. (See how that joke book on page 3 keeps coming in handy?)

PAY ATTENTION TO OTHER PEOPLE

If you want someone's attention, give them yours! Ask them how their day was. Ask them if they think dolphins are creepy. Ask them about themselves, and they'll probably return the favor!

50

THINGS
TO DO WHEN
YOU'RE BORED

By the time you've finished this book,
you should never be bored again!

1. MAKE POPSICLES

2. PRANK YOUR PARENTS

3. GO FOR A WALK

4. PRACTICE YOUR "INNOCENT FACE"

5. TAKE AN AMAZING BATH

6. HELP SOMEONE OUT

7. GO TO THE LIBRARY

8. START A LEMONADE STAND

9. MAKE A TIME CAPSULE

10. SCARE BUGS WITH GUM

11. PRACTICE TREADING WATER

12. MAKE A FLOWER BOUQUET

13. LEARN A FEW JOKES

14. CHALLENGE SOMEONE TO A CONTEST

15. SEARCH FOR FAIRIES OR GNOMES

16. START PLANNING YOUR HALLOWEEN COSTUME

17. PUT ON LAST YEAR'S COSTUME AND SCARE THE NEIGHBORS

18. READ A BOOK

19. WRITE A STORY

20. HAVE A DANCE PARTY

21. CLEAN YOUR ROOM

22. MAKE SOME ART

23. WORK ON YOUR DISGUISES

24. HAVE A PHOTO SHOOT WITH YOUR PET

25. LOOK FOR ANIMAL TRACKS

26. DO A GOOD DEED

27. MAKE FAKE BOOGERS

28. PLAY HIDE-AND-SEEK

29. DO A SCIENCE EXPERIMENT

30. READ ABOUT BIGFOOT

31. LEARN SOME INTERESTING FACTS

32. PICK YOUR FAVORITE OUTFITS

33. DISCOVER NEW USES FOR GUM

34. BUILD AN AWESOME FORT

35. DRAW A MAP OF YOUR NEIGHBORHOOD

36. HAVE A BIKE RACE

37. DO A FEW CHORES

38. GET SOME EXERCISE

39. TELL SCARY STORIES

40. COME UP WITH NEW USES FOR FAKE MUSTACHES

41. TRY A FOOD YOU USED TO HATE

42. MAKE BALLOON SWORDS

43. TEACH YOUR PET WEIRD TRICKS

44. SNEAK AROUND THE HOUSE

45. HAVE SQUIRT GUN TARGET PRACTICE

46. FIND THE PERFECT HIDING SPOT

47. PLAY BRAIN GAMES

48. JOIN A CLUB

49. GET YOUR REVENGE

50. DISCOVER YOUR HIDDEN POWERS

YOUR HIDDEN POWERS CHECKLIST

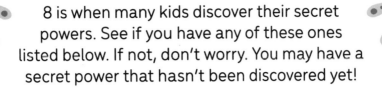

8 is when many kids discover their secret powers. See if you have any of these ones listed below. If not, don't worry. You may have a secret power that hasn't been discovered yet!

I CAN:

- ☐ LICK MY OWN ELBOW
- ☐ BEND A SPOON USING ONLY MY MIND
- ☐ PUT MY FEET BEHIND MY HEAD
- ☐ TALK TO ANIMALS (BUT THEY DON'T TALK BACK)
- ☐ TALK TO ANIMALS (THEY DO TALK BACK)
- ☐ MOVE THROUGH THE HOUSE WITHOUT BEING HEARD
- ☐ MAKE PEOPLE PEE THEIR PANTS LAUGHING
- ☐ DO A SPLIT
- ☐ SEE IN THE DARK
- ☐ GET A DOG TO FOLLOW ME WHEREVER I GO
- ☐ RUN SUPER FAST

- ☐ JUMP SUPER HIGH
- ☐ READ OTHER PEOPLE'S MINDS
- ☐ BE INVISIBLE
- ☐ WIGGLE MY EARS
- ☐ MAKE BABIES STOP CRYING
- ☐ SOLVE REALLY HARD MATH PROBLEMS
- ☐ TELL AMAZING STORIES
- ☐ WRITE IN CURSIVE
- ☐ SEE FARTHER THAN GROWN-UPS
- ☐ CHANGE A PARENT'S MOOD FROM GOOD TO BAD
- ☐ CHANGE A PARENT'S MOOD FROM BAD TO GOOD
- ☐ FREEZE THINGS WITH MY BREATH

How To Make NEW FRIENDS

When I was your age, I had to change schools.
That meant making a whole new set of friends.
For some kids, making new friends is super easy.
But I was shy, and the whole thing felt very scary.

If only I had known how easy it can be!
Here's what you've got to do:

GO UP AND SAY HI!

Sometimes it's easier to make new friends one at a time. All you have to do is look for a kid who's doing something interesting. Maybe they're playing a game you like, or reading a book you love. Maybe they're studying wild animal prints in the playground, or building a rocket to Mars. If it looks like fun, see if you can join them! (If they say no, don't get upset. Just keep looking!)

ASK PEOPLE ABOUT THEMSELVES

One of the best ways to make friends is to find people who love some of the same things you do. How do you know what someone loves? Ask them! What kind of games do they like to play? What kind of music do they listen to? How do they feel about poop? What's their favorite book? What kind of ice cream makes them drool?

DO THINGS YOU BOTH LIKE

Once you find out what you have in common, do the things you love together!

JOIN A CLUB OR A TEAM

Want to meet other kids who love tracking animals? Join the Scouts! Want to hang out with people who live for basketball? Join a team! And if you can't find a club or a team you want to join, why not try to start one?

HERE ARE A FEW THINGS YOU *SHOULDN'T DO:*

- Don't expect a friend to do everything you want to do. That's not how friendship works!

- Don't bug people. If someone doesn't want to play, that's fine! Just ask again later. If they say no again, ask someone else!

- Don't spend time with people who are mean to you.

- Don't spend time with people who are mean to other kids.

- Don't be mean. Otherwise people won't want to spend time with you!

A FEW THINGS YOU SHOULD KNOW IF YOU'RE SHY

I was really, really shy when I was 8. I know how hard it can be! I also know how annoying it is when people keep telling you, "Don't be shy!"

So I'm not going to say that. But I will tell you a few things that I hope will make you feel a little more comfortable. If they don't, it's OK. Just keep in mind that even super shy kids can grow up to be confident, wise-cracking adults like me!

NO ONE'S PAYING AS MUCH ATTENTION AS YOU THINK

I know it can feel like everyone's staring at you. But I promise, they're not. They're probably thinking about what they're going to have for lunch—or trying their best not to fart in public.

A SMILE CAN GO A LONG WAY

Too nervous to talk? Smile instead! A smile will tell people you're friendly. Maybe they'll do the hard work and come over to say hi to you! If you need some help smiling, just think about the things you love the most, like sloppy kisses from your dog—or chocolate-covered ice cream cones.

A LOT OF OTHER KIDS ARE SHY, TOO!

You can probably spot the shy kids if you look for them. Go say hi! I'm pretty sure they would love to meet you, too.

IT'S OK TO GO SLOW

Ask questions and get people talking about themselves. It will give you more time to get comfortable.

YOU ARE AWESOME

And everyone will figure that out as soon as they get to know you!

WHAT TO DO iF YOU GET iN TROUBLE AT SCHOOL

I'm sure you're the best-behaved kid in the whole wide world. (Wink, wink.) That doesn't mean you won't get in trouble some day. I definitely did! (Just ask my mom.)

So you've been nabbed by a teacher, principal, or cafeteria monitor. What you need to do next depends on how you answer these 3 questions:

DiD YOU DO iT?

I don't know what it was. Hopefully it wasn't too terrible! At your age, you probably should have known better. But don't worry—this isn't the beginning of a life of crime!

The first thing you should do is come clean. Admit that you're guilty. The second thing you need to do is apologize. Saying you're sorry—and meaning it—may make your punishment a little less painful.

DiD YOU HAVE A GOOD REASON FOR DOiNG iT?

Let's say you got caught running through the halls with a hot dog you stole from the cafeteria. But that's only part of the story. You were actually rushing to get the hot dog to a starving raccoon baby you found in the schoolyard. So you had a good reason for doing what you did! Will it get you out of trouble? I have no idea. But it can't hurt to make sure everyone knows.

ARE YOU AN iNNOCENT ANGEL?

If you've gotten into trouble for something you didn't do, you have to stand up for yourself! Don't yell. Don't cry. Don't kick your backpack or throw your pencil on the ground. Stay calm and tell your side of the story. If there are other people who know you're telling the truth, get them to say so! (These are called witnesses.)

I wish I could promise you that the truth will always get you out of trouble, but I'm afraid that's not the case. Sometimes innocent people get punished. It's not fair, but that's life.

UH-OH. SOMETHING TERRIBLE JUST HAPPENED.

WHAT SHOULD YOU DO?

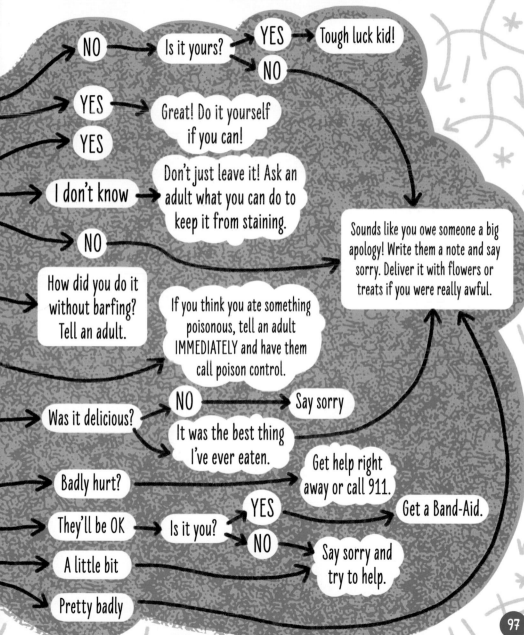

NO → Is it yours? → YES → Tough luck kid!

NO

YES → Great! Do it yourself if you can!

YES

I don't know → Don't just leave it! Ask an adult what you can do to keep it from staining.

NO

How did you do it without barfing? Tell an adult.

If you think you ate something poisonous, tell an adult IMMEDIATELY and have them call poison control.

Sounds like you owe someone a big apology! Write them a note and say sorry. Deliver it with flowers or treats if you were really awful.

Was it delicious? → NO → Say sorry

It was the best thing I've ever eaten.

Badly hurt? → Get help right away or call 911.

They'll be OK → Is it you? → YES → Get a Band-Aid.

NO

A little bit

Say sorry and try to help.

Pretty badly

97

WHAT'S 911, AND WHEN SHOULD YOU CALL iT?

Have you heard about 911?
That's the phone number you're supposed
to call when there's an emergency.

When you dial 911, a person will ask you what the emergency is. Tell them what's happened! They will also ask where you are. If you know the address, give it to them. If not, stay on the phone and they may be able to find you.

CALL 911 IF SOMEONE IS REALLY HURT

If a person is bleeding badly or isn't able to talk, call 911 immediately.

DON'T CALL IF SOMEONE NEEDS A BAND-AID

If you can take care of it by yourself, there's no need to call 911.

IF THERE'S A FIRE, GET TO SAFETY FIRST, THEN CALL

If you are in a building that is on fire, the first thing you need to do is GET OUT. Don't stop to call 911. Call as soon as you are outside and no longer in danger.

CALL 911 IF AN ADULT TRIES TO HURT YOU

Find a safe place and call right away.

DON'T CALL 911 IF YOU'RE BORED OR YOU WANT TO SEE WHAT WILL HAPPEN

No, no, no. Calling 911 when you're bored is a VERY bad idea. While someone is answering your call, a person who really needs help could be trying to get through! You can get in big trouble if you call 911 for no reason, and I'm afraid this book won't be able to help you!

6 AMAZiNG THiNGS YOU CAN DO WiTH GUM

Chewing gum is one of the most wonderful things on Earth. Can you think of anything else that can freshen your breath *and* make a great fake booger? Yeah, I didn't think so.

But that's not all chewing gum is able to do!

TRICK SNEAKY FRIENDS

Popping other people's bubbles is one of the best things about being 8. (When you're a grown-up, people think you're weird when you do it!) The next time you're with a friend who likes to stick his/her fingers into your bubbles, here's what to do: Blow a big bubble. Then take it out of your mouth and put it in the freezer. As soon as it's frozen hard, put the gum back in your mouth with the bubble sticking out and let your sneaky friend try their best to pop it!

PICK UP THINGS YOU CAN'T
(OR DON'T WANT TO) TOUCH

Did you drop something where you can't reach it? Just find a long stick and put a piece of well-chewed gum on the end. Then go fishing! This works for things you don't want to touch, too!

SCARE BUGS AND CATCH CRABS

I've heard that some bugs hate the smell of spearmint gum. Which bugs? Go find out! This is your science experiment for today! Bugs may hate spearmint gum, but I've heard that crabs LOVE it. Next time you're at the beach, see how many you can catch!

FiX BROKEN STUFF

Let's say you broke something (like your glasses or your aunt's favorite vase). You need to fix it fast, but you don't have any glue! A little piece of chewing gum can stick it back together long enough for you to buy some glue—or flee the country.

STICK THINGS WHERE YOU WANT THEM

You never know when you'll want to stick a secret message to the bottom of a drawer—or a note to a wall. You can't carry tape and glue around with you wherever you go. But you can slip a piece of gum in your pocket, no problem!

WHAT TO DO iF YOU'RE HAViNG A TERRiBLE DAY

Everything has gone wrong! A dog peed on your shoes on the way to school. You left your homework in your bedroom. And to top it all off, you farted in front of your entire class!

You're having the worst day EVER. What are you going to do?

TELL SOMEONE

Talking about your problems can make you feel better. Is there someone you trust who's good at listening? It could be a friend, a parent, or a brother or sister. Tell them about all of the things that have gone wrong. They might be able to help! But even if they can't, you'll be glad you got it all out.

TRY YOUR BEST TO LAUGH

Sometimes a having a good laugh is the best thing you can do. Sure, having a dog pee on your shoes is awful when it happens, but after a while it might start to seem funny. If you can laugh at your problems, it's a lot easier to make some of them go away.

HA! HA! HA!

SCREAM YOUR GUTS OUT

Some things just aren't funny. When I can't laugh at my problems, I like to scream. I go into my bedroom, grab one of my pillows, press it against my face, and scream into it. If you do it right, the pillow will keep your scream from being too loud. I know it's weird, but it makes me feel better!

GET SOME EXERCISE

Exercise is great when you're mad. Throw a basketball against a wall outside. Run as fast as you can. Dance until you drop. It will help you get all the bad feelings out.

GO TO BED EARLY

A good night's sleep can make everything better. And if your day's been awful, you might as well end it! Tomorrow is going to be soooooo much better!

MORE THINGS THAT CAN MAKE BAD DAYS A BIT BETTER

Sitting in the sunshine

Cuddling your pets

Doing a good deed

Taking a nap

Going outside for a walk

Having a friend over to play

Tickle time

Getting hugs

Taking a bath

Reading a funny book

Watching a great movie

8

MOViES
8-YEAR-OLDS
LOVE

1. THE PRINCESS BRIDE

2. HARRY POTTER AND
THE SORCERER'S STONE

3. THE INCREDIBLES

4. MY NEIGHBOR TOTORO

5. E.T. THE EXTRA-TERRESTRIAL

6. THE MUPPET MOVIE

7. MATILDA

8. WALLACE AND GROMIT:
THE CURSE OF THE WERE RABBIT

WHERE TO HUNT FOR

FAiRiES

OR

GNOMES

Adults will tell you there are no such things as fairies or gnomes. They're right. For adults, magical creatures don't exist. But when you're 8 years old, you can believe in whatever you like. And fairies and gnomes are *much* more likely to show themselves to people who believe in them.

You don't need to set off into the woods to hunt for fairies or gnomes. All you need are sharp eyes. If you look around, you can see signs of these creatures everywhere. But if you're lucky enough to spot a fairy or gnome, don't try to catch it! They're not always nice!

Here are a few signs that there are fairies or gnomes are around . . .

YOUR PETS ARE ACTING STRANGE

Is your cat always watching something out the window—something you can't see? Does your dog ever bolt across the park all of the sudden or bark for no reason? They may have seen or smelled a fairy or gnome.

WEIRD PLANTS OR FLOWERS HAVE SPROUTED

Have you ever found a flower or plant in your garden or yard that doesn't seem to belong there? It may have been planted by a magical creature. If so, don't pick it! Keep an eye on it and wait for its owner to come back.

YOU FIND MUSHROOMS GROWING IN A CIRCLE

A ring of mushrooms is called a "fairy circle" for a reason. This is where fairies come to dance.

LITTLE SPARKLY THINGS KEEP GOING MISSING

Fairies will often "borrow" pretty little things like rings and rhinestones. Leave a few sparkly things on your windowsill and see if a fairy will pay you a visit. (Just don't expect to get your stuff back if a fairy decides to take it!)

YOU SPOT A HOLE AT THE BASE OF A TREE

Gnomes like to build their homes beneath big, old trees. The hole you've found could be a secret entrance. Have a look, but don't stick your fingers inside. When gnomes move out, snakes can move in.

HOW TO GET MAD

OMG why do you need this dumb chapter!
You don't need to be told how to get mad!
It happens all the time!

It's natural to get mad when someone's done something wrong. But do you want to stay mad for the rest of your life? If so, you can turn the page right now! But if you want things to get better, keep reading.

TAKE A DEEP BREATH

Count to 10 if it helps. Do your best not to yell, scream, or cry. Sure, yelling can feel satisfying, but it's not going do you much good. If you want people to understand you, it's best to speak in a normal voice.

TRY TO SEE THE OTHER SIDE

Why did the person do what they did? Were they being a jerk? Was it an accident? Is there a chance that they had a good reason? Figuring it out might make you feel a little less angry.

TELL THE PERSON WHY YOU'RE MAD

If you don't tell them, how will they know? Maybe they don't even realize they hurt your feelings or stepped on your toe or dripped popsicle juice all over your shirt!

LET THEM KNOW WHAT WOULD FIX THINGS

Most of us don't like it when other people are mad at us. We'll do what we can to make things better! So tell them what they can do—or at least give them a chance to say sorry!

TAKE A BREAK

If none of this works, and you're still angry, walk away and spend a little time alone. Sometimes that's the only thing that works.

FAKE SPIDERS

THE BEST REVENGE

You're going to get mad a million times in your life. Whenever you can, you should try to forgive or forget. When you just can't do it, no matter how hard you try, that's when it's time for fake spiders.

Fake spiders are so much better than fights or arguments. Only use them when you're really, really mad. All you have to do is leave a few where the person who messed with you is likely to find them. I recommend:

SHOES

UNDERWEAR DRAWERS

LUNCHBOXES

 TOILETS

COAT POCKETS

BACKPACKS

PENCIL CASES

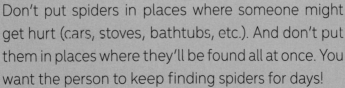
Don't put spiders in places where someone might get hurt (cars, stoves, bathtubs, etc.). And don't put them in places where they'll be found all at once. You want the person to keep finding spiders for days!

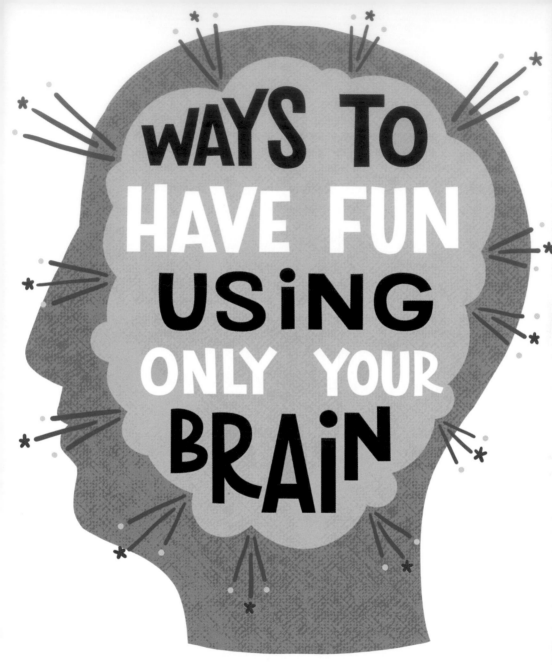

WAYS TO HAVE FUN USING ONLY YOUR BRAIN

When I was a kid, we had no screens. I know it must sound like torture to many of you, but I promise, we kept ourselves well entertained.

When we were in the car, we played games like "I Spy" or tried to spot license plates from every state. But the best games of all were the ones we played using our imaginations.

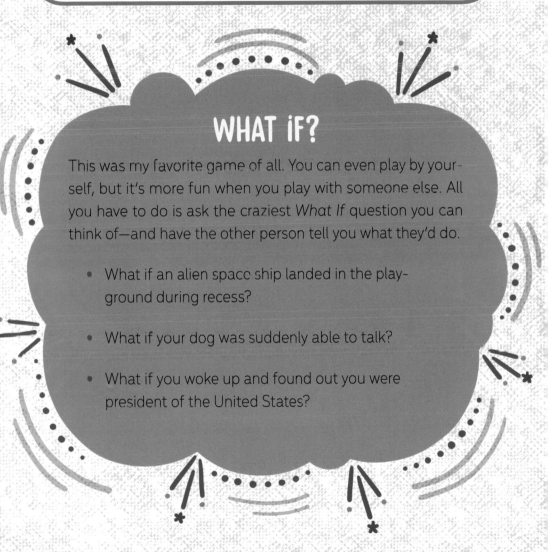

WHAT iF?

This was my favorite game of all. You can even play by yourself, but it's more fun when you play with someone else. All you have to do is ask the craziest *What If* question you can think of—and have the other person tell you what they'd do.

- What if an alien space ship landed in the playground during recess?

- What if your dog was suddenly able to talk?

- What if you woke up and found out you were president of the United States?

WOULD YOU RATHER?

Another all-time favorite! It's super simple to play. You come up with 2 weird tasks and your friend has to choose which one they'd rather do.

- Would you rather wrestle a grizzly bear or be stuck in a room with a dozen snakes?

- Would you rather wear your bathing suit to school or sing "Baby Shark" to strangers in the middle of town?

- Would you rather have the ability to fly or the ability to breathe under water?

WHAT'S GROSSER?

Same idea, just with super gross stuff. I think you know what I'm talking about.

- What's grosser? Eating a rotten egg or eating a giant booger?

CHANGE THAT SONG

Is there a song that you know all the words to? Wouldn't it be so much better if it was all about you and your friends? Just make up new lyrics and you'll have your own theme song!

HOW TO GET DRESSED

By now, you're probably picking out most of the clothes you wear. Some kids love getting dressed in the morning. Some would rather stay in their pajamas.

But the truth is, you're going to be doing this for the rest of your life, so you might as well learn how to do it right!

IF IT'S TOO SMALL OR COVERED IN MUSTARD, DON'T WEAR IT

Nothing looks good with dirt, magic marker, or last night's spaghetti sauce on it. And if it's too small or large, you're going to be miserable by the end of the day. Wear something that makes you comfortable and confident. You gotta feel good to look good!

DECIDE WHETHER YOU'D RATHER STAND OUT OR BLEND IN

It's up to you! Maybe you're the kind of kid who loves lots of attention. In that case, pick out an outfit that no one else will be rocking. But if you're the kind of person who'd rather blend in, that's great, too!

DON'T WEAR A PARKA TO A POOL PARTY

This is important! You don't want to ruin a fancy dress by wearing it on a hike. Or freeze your butt off in a pair of swim trunks at a hockey game. Pick out an outfit that's going to make you feel good wherever you're going.

LOOK FOR PEOPLE WHO LOOK GOOD TO YOU

Is there someone you know who always looks amazing? It doesn't matter if it's another kid or an adult. Go ahead and ask for advice! Most people will be super flattered that you like their style.

JUST BE YOU

The most important thing is to wear stuff that makes you feel great. If you put on an outfit, and it makes you feel like you could take over the world—that's the right outfit.

HOW TO PICK YOUR FAVORITE OUTFIT

Not sure what looks good on you?
Go ahead and try everything on!

Go through your dresser and see what's in there. I bet there's stuff tucked away that you forgot you own! If you have older siblings, see if they have anything that doesn't fit anymore. It's the next best thing to going shopping!

TRY LOTS OF DIFFERENT COMBINATIONS

Sometimes you don't know what looks good until you see yourself in the mirror.

TAKE PICTURES!

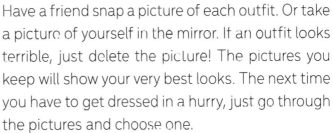

Have a friend snap a picture of each outfit. Or take a picture of yourself in the mirror. If an outfit looks terrible, just delete the picture! The pictures you keep will show your very best looks. The next time you have to get dressed in a hurry, just go through the pictures and choose one.

GET RID OF STUFF YOU DON'T WEAR ANYMORE

Unless it's ruined, don't throw it out! Give stuff that's too small to someone younger and smaller! If you have clothes that just bore you, why not ask your friends if they have stuff they'd like to trade. Swap clothes, and everyone will feel like they got something new!

SHARE!

WHAT TO DO IF YOU'RE NOT THRILLED ABOUT BEING THE TALLEST, SHORTEST, BIGGEST, OR SMALLEST KID IN YOUR CLASS

I know exactly what it's like. When I was your age, I was the shortest kid in my class—and I did *not* love it.

If you feel a bit weird about being the tallest/shortest/biggest/smallest, here's what I would suggest.

1. USE YOUR SUPERPOWERS

You think you're different. But have you ever considered that you might be *special*? Maybe you've noticed that you can do things other kids can't. If you're the smallest, you can fit into places other kids can't go. If you're the tallest, you can reach things the others can't reach. If you're the biggest, you may also be the strongest, too. So instead of feeling bad, why not feel proud? I bet a lot of those other kids would love to be able to do what you do!

Not convinced?

2. JUST WAIT

You may not be the tallest/shortest/biggest/smallest kid for long! The kids in your class are growing and changing every day—and so are you. It's hard to know what any of you will look like next year! Everybody grows at their own pace. When I was 8, I was the shortest. But by the time I was 12, I was right in the middle! (And I kind of missed my superpowers!)

HOW TO MAKE A TIME CAPSULE

In the future, other kids will wonder what it was like to be 8 right now. By making a time capsule, you can show them!

Before the year is over, find a big glass jar (like the ones spaghetti sauce comes in). Clean it out well and take off the label. Fill it with all sorts of things that will help future kids know what life was like in the olden days.

HERE ARE SOME IDEAS

- This year's school photo
- A letter to the future kids. Tell them who you are and what your life is like!
- One of your art projects
- A small toy
- A souvenir from a trip you took
- A list of predictions. What do you think life will be like for kids your age in 100 years?
- A picture of your neighborhood
- A trading card (like Pokémon)
- Your favorite popsicle recipe
- A tiny squirt gun
- A fake spider

DON'T ADD

- Anything that will rot (like food)
- Anything you're going to need
- Anything valuable
- Anything that doesn't belong to you

When you've finished filling your time capsule, bury it where it won't be disturbed for a very long time!

9 THiNGS YOU SHOULD DO BEFORE YOU TURN 9

(iF YOU HAVEN'T ALREADY)

☐ MEMORIZE YOUR ADDRESS AND YOUR PARENTS' PHONE NUMBERS

☐ PICK 2 CHORES YOU CAN DO TO HELP OUT AROUND YOUR HOUSE— AND DO THEM!

☐ KNOW HOW TO TELL TIME USING A CLOCK THAT HAS HANDS (INSTEAD OF NUMBERS)

☐ FIGURE OUT HOW TO MAKE CHANGE USING DOLLARS AND COINS

☐ HOP ON A BIKE AND RIDE LIKE THE WIND

☐ IF YOU CAN GET TO A POOL, LEARN HOW TO SWIM, FLOAT, AND TREAD WATER

☐ GO OUT OF YOUR WAY TO DO ONE NICE THING FOR ANOTHER PERSON EVERY WEEK

☐ READ A BOOK WITHOUT PICTURES (OR A JUST A FEW LITTLE ONES). IF YOU FINISH THIS BOOK, IT COUNTS!

☐ WRITE A BEAUTIFUL APOLOGY LETTER—'CAUSE IF YOU HAVEN'T DONE SOMETHING WRONG, IT'S BEEN A PRETTY BORING YEAR!

WHY THE NEXT TWO YEARS ARE GOING TO BE AWESOME AWESOME AWESOME AWESOME

8 is great, but so are years 9 and 10!
Here are a few things you can look forward to!

BEING TALL ENOUGH TO RIDE ROLLER COASTERS

USING THE OVEN OR MICROWAVE (IF YOU CAN PROVE YOU'RE SUPER MATURE)

DECORATING YOUR OWN ROOM

BEING FAST ENOUGH TO ESCAPE FROM UNWANTED HUGS

MAKING YOUR OWN MONEY

SPENDING YOUR OWN MONEY

SITTING IN THE FRONT SEAT OF THE CAR

HANGING OUT WITH YOUR FRIENDS— WITHOUT ADULTS WATCHING

BIGGER FEET

ACKNOWLEDGMENTS

This series began as a birthday present for my daughter, Georgia, and her best friend, Wyatt. I owe Wyatt and his mom, Stephanie Kim Simons, my eternal gratitude for their friendship, enthusiasm, and encouragement.

Thanks as always to Suzanne Gluck and Andrea Blatt at WME for their tireless support. Andrea deserves a medal—or maybe a statue built in her honor. For now, I hope this acknowledgment will suffice!

This series would not have been possible without Anne Heltzel at Abrams, who shared my vision from the very beginning, and Hana Nakamura, who brought that vision to life.

And thanks to Michael Buckley, the funniest man on earth and one of the few adults who know how to enjoy life like a 10-year-old.

ABOUT THE AUTHOR

KIRSTEN MILLER is a renowned author of middle-grade and YA fiction. She lives in Brooklyn with her precocious 10-year-old, who helped write this book. Find out more at kirstenmillerbooks.com.

DON'T FORGET TO CHECK OUT

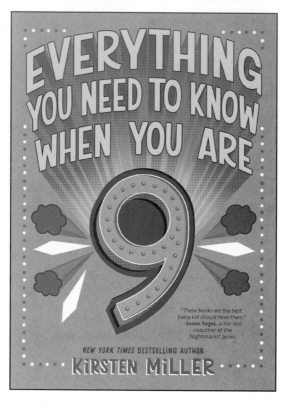

EVERYTHING YOU NEED TO KNOW WHEN YOU ARE 9

"These books are the best. Every kid should have them."
—**Jason Segel**, actor and coauthor of the Nightmares! series

NEW YORK TIMES BESTSELLING AUTHOR
KiRSTEN MiLLER

FOR ALL THE BEST SECRETS ABOUT TURNING 9!